Adult Coloring Book Series

The Mystical Mandala Coloring Book

50 Mandala Designs For Stress Relief, Relaxation and Art Therapy (Volume 3)

Michelle Shea

A Note From The Author

Thank you for purchasing The Mystical Mandala Coloring Book.

Beginning at the next page you will find 50 mandala illustrations for your coloring pleasure. The 50 mandalas in this volume is a mix of simple and more intricate drawings to suit a range of preferences.

This book is part of the Adult Coloring Book Series-Mandalas. If you enjoy this book, please take a look at the other coloring titles at the back cover of this book. You will certainly find plenty of outstanding coloring pages to keep you active and entertained.

You will notice that there is just one design per page and the back is left blank. This is done on purpose so that should the colors bleed through to the back page, they do not ruin the mandalas.

You may wish to put a thin sheet of cardboard between pages to prevent the ink from bleeding through to the following pages when using gel pens or markers to do your coloring. Or you could choose coloring utensils like pencils that will not bleed through the paper. Do be aware however that if you press a hard tipped surface to the page, such as when using a ball-point pen, it may leave a depression on the page behind your current coloring surface.

With these thoughts in mind, I urge you to get ready your pencils, crayons, markers or whatever you prefer to color or paint in and have a great time coloring the pages in this book.

Before I leave, I have a quick favor to ask and will appreciate if you please take **one minute** to leave a **personal review** of this book on the sales page. It is a fact that my future success as a coloring book author is directly tied to the number of people talking about my books and it is my sincerest hope that you will find my books worthy of your recommendations. Do take time to **post pictures of your colored mandalas** on the **Amazon review page** for us to ogle and admire!

If you have any questions or fancy a chat, do drop me an email at michelle@amzndownload.com

Enjoy coloring.

Sincerely yours,
Michelle Shea

MY1

MY2

MY3

MY4

MY5

MY6

MY7

MY8

MY9

MY10

MY11

MY12

MY13

MY14

MY15

MY16

MY17

MY18

MY19

MY20

MY21

MY22

MY23

MY24

MY25

MY26

MY27

MY28

MY29

MY30

MY31

MY32

MY33

MY34

MY35

MY36

MY37

MY38

MY39

MY40

MY41

MY42

MY43

MY44

MY45

MY46

MY47

MY48

MY49

MY50

HERE IS A SECRET GIFT FOR YOU

If I could personally thank everyone who bought my book I really would, but unfortunately that is just not possible. However, I do try my best to show my appreciation with **newsletter exclusive free mandalas** and **limited time coupons** (for purchases of my other coloring books) for those who subscribe to my secret newsletter and follow me on this wonderful coloring and design journey.

So, would you do me the honor of subscribing to my newsletter? It is **completely free** and within a few days you will receive some great free downloads including **special mandalas** from my secret collection straight into your inbox! These mandalas will never be published as they are exclusive to my newsletter subscribers only. And I think you will love the mandalas!

I will also be sending you fun and useful reading on mandalas and coloring. Once in a while, I also organise super exciting coloring competitions and giveaways via my newsletter which means there is more coloring goodies to be won.

So, just click on the link below, fill out your name and email address so I know where to send you my first newsletter and get you started on this amazing coloring journey.

http://mandala.amzndownload.com

Thank you so much and see you soon!

Michelle Shea